# William Taylor

# William Taylor

## A Portrait of a Pioneer Prophet

*John Erik Aho*

iUniverse, Inc.
New York  Lincoln  Shanghai

**William Taylor**
A Portrait of a Pioneer Prophet

iUniverse, Inc.

For information address:
iUniverse
2021 Pine Lake Road, Suite 100
Lincoln, NE 68512
www.iuniverse.com

ISBN: 0-595-29134-1

Printed in the United States of America

# Contents

# Foreword

By
Jay Kesler, President Emeritus
Taylor University
September 2003

I'm certain that the students, faculty and alumni of Taylor University as well as a host of fellow Christians interested in missionary biography will include this short, readable but thorough treatment of the life and ministry of William Taylor in their reading. I have often wondered at the relative lack of exposure that this great evangelist has received in church history. One reason, I am sure, is that there is no twentieth century mission society that traces its founding to Taylor and thus no sponsor for a definitive history. His indigenous methods were ahead of the times and thus often opposed by official policies.

John Aho has done us all a service by preserving much information gleaned from the many out of print books by and about William Taylor. The Methodist College founded in Fort Wayne, Indiana in 1846 adopted his name during the height of his popularity in 1890 as a tribute to his vision and missionary passion with the fond hope that students would be inspired to follow his footsteps and indeed the intent has been realized far beyond their prayers and expectations. This short volume will contribute to keeping the flame burning brightly in the future.

Taylor was born while Thomas Jefferson was still living and ministered, traveled, wrote, inspired and preached into the presidency of Theodore Roosevelt. He continued his pursuit of the "great commission" through the frontier period of Andrew Jackson, James K. Polk, "Manifest Destiny", the Mexican War, the Oregon Trail, fifty four forty or fight, Abraham Lincoln, the Civil War, reconstruction, the Little Bighorn and almost to Kitty Hawk. Yet interest in his exploits did not waiver and he was able to largely support himself and his ministries through the sale of his books. "California Taylor" documented the gold rush of 1849 to curious easterners and with insight far ahead of his time challenged the idea of "colonial missions" by advocating "Pauline missions" led by indigenous people in every continent he visited. This is a timely heroic story, and to think that it took place mostly before steamships, on horse or mule, often by foot to some of the most difficult places on the globe. It has been my experience to visit many of the locations where William Taylor ministered in India, South America, Australia and Northern Africa—not in 19th century mode but by jet airplane, car, Landrover, bus or truck. Recently I drove from the San Francisco airport to the Mount Hermon Christian Conference facility and looked out toward the Pacific across the densely populated bay area and realized that before there were any towns, only a few scattered miners cabins, William Taylor walked with backpack from family to family to share the gospel in the rugged terrain.

As I have traveled these places I marvel at the courage, vision and faithfulness of pioneer missionaries like William Taylor and pray that this book will in its own way inspire 21st century youth to heroic efforts as they meet modern challenges.

# Introduction

# A Methodist at a Baptist Seminary

My wife, Michelle, and I graduated from Taylor University in 1992 not knowing much about our school's namesake. William Taylor was a man who touched the lives of thousands from the early gold rush days to the turn of the 20<sup>th</sup> century, but was also a man who touched my life in a profound way.

I was still a member of First United Methodist Church in Plymouth, Michigan, when I started taking seminary courses at Golden Gate Baptist Theological Seminary in Mill Valley, California.

While I was at Golden Gate I took a class called Great Preachers with Dr. Craig Skinner, who himself authored a biography of Charles Spurgeon and his son Thomas called *Lamplighter and Son*. He suggested two preachers to do research on. He mentioned William Sangster, from London, and William Taylor. I asked Dr. Skinner whether he knew I graduated from Taylor University and he said he did not. This began my study into the life of this pioneer prophet.

We hear of Taylor's contemporary, D.L. Moody, much more than we hear of Taylor. And yet Taylor was asked to come join Moody in London. Taylor worked on five continents not only as an evangelist, but also as a pastor, author, publisher, missionary, educator, and church planter. What struck me most about him was not so much his accomplishments, but his heart. He had an unquenchable desire to reach out to others with God's love.

Throughout his life he realized how God's hand was on him. "I see more and more clearly that it is too late for me to begin to make plans for the Lord by which to work, when God has so long ago made plans for me. It is not mine to ask him to indorse my plans and go with me, but by all available means to discern his plans and go with him."

I hope in painting this portrait that you will live with the purpose and passion of this pioneer prophet.

"I became more and more convinced that a great work of God
was what Calcutta least desired and most needed,
and that a more convenient season would never come;
so I determined, as the Lord should lead, to push the battle and win or die at
the guns....
God has sent me here to organize at least one body of witnessing soldiers for Jesus
who will endure hardness; and by the power of the Holy Spirit
I must succeed or die in the trenches of the enemy.
God help me! It is for thy glory and the salvation of these poor, perishing millions,
in love and pity for whom my Saviour died."—William Taylor, 1872

# Chapter One

## Early Life

The shot was fired, marking the beginning of the Revolutionary War. Five brothers—James, William, John and Canfield Taylor—fought for the freedom of America beginning in 1775. Little did James know that his grandson would fight for peoples' freedom across five continents, in a *very* different war.

James Taylor married a daughter of a revolutionary Captain by the name of Audley Paul. Paul was a fellow lieutenant of George Washington and was present when Washington made a suggestion to General Braddock. He thought that the soldiers should be allowed to fight from within the cover of the trees. Braddock, in a condescending tone, called Washington a young Buckskin, thinking his idea was ridiculous. This took place on the morning of the battle known as "Braddock's Defeat."

The Pauls were staunchly opposed to slavery, a belief that was passed down to the rising generation of Taylors. As fast as the younger Taylors inherited the slaves, they were set free. This trend of setting slaves free would be carried out in the Taylor family, as a new born baby would grow up to be in the business of setting people free.

# An Encounter

William Taylor was born in Rockbridge, Virginia on May 2, 1821. He was born to Stuart and Martha Taylor who were Presbyterians in faith. In recalling the memory of his parents, he said that they had practical common sense and had energy well above the average. Stuart was a tanner and currier by trade. He grew up on a farm, where he grew as a man with an incredible mind for mechanics.

Thinking that faith was a set of standards to follow, Stuart and Martha tried to live up to their church's standards for thirteen years. William felt that his parents had the form of godliness, but they lacked the power. However, Stuart Taylor realized faith was more than a religion. It was a relationship. At a Methodist Camp Meeting, Stuart started dealing with things he had done in his past.

One day, young William went hunting with his father, but the furthest thing from Stuart's mind was the hunt itself. He was so convicted by his sins that he contemplated suicide. Stuart spent most of the day, sitting beneath an old chestnut tree weeping, with his son looking on. A few weeks later, another camp meeting was started at Cold Sulfur Springs. Driving a herd of cattle toward the place of the meeting, Stuart stopped "to see what's going on at the camp meeting." He went back to that meeting for three days straight before he made his way down front to the altar.

With tears trailing down his face, Stuart cried out, "God have mercy on me, a poor sinner. Oh God, for Christ's sake, have mercy on me a poor sinner." After fifteen minutes of "piling up his short prayers 'til they reached heaven," God answered, "Son, your sins are forgiven."

Stuart returned home to express his excitement to his son: "William, I am converted." He began to laugh and cried out, "Yes William, I am converted to God…God bless the Methodists." Recalling to his wife what had happened, Stuart gathered the family together to read the Bible and give thanks to God for what He had done.

His father became a witness to his world. He brought his family to the meeting and was so concerned about those around him. He rode throughout town on his horse, gathering all the elders of the church as well as other leading members to ask when they were "born again" and why they had not told him about it. Instead of joining in his excitement, the leaders reported to others how Stuart Taylor had "scandalized himself and his church, at the Methodist camp meeting, and had gone crazy."

# Humor Me

Young William's childhood was full of fun and games, or so he thought. His sense of humor made him less of an angel at school. Recalling his time at one school, Taylor said that he "laughed and talked too much for the good discipline of the institution." He tended to set "the school to laughing" on many occasions, a tool that would be of use in his later years of preaching in the streets.

As early as seven or eight, William worked on his father's farm six days a week. He learned the lessons of hard work early, which gave him little time "for getting into mischief." As a child, he was often called on to read the New Testament for visitors. He was taught by his parents to read Scripture, and his mother taught him to sing hymns. Through this, he felt convicted of his sins, but did not know how to go to God:

> But soon after, as I sat one night in the corner by the kitchen fire, the Spirit of the Lord came on me, and I found myself suddenly weeping aloud, and confessing my sins in detail, as I could recall them, to God, and begged Him, for Jesus' sake to forgive them, with all I could not remember; and I found myself trusting in Jesus that it would all be so, and, in a few minutes, my heart was filled with peace and love, not the shadow of doubt remaining. I was fully conscious of having been forgiven, and received "a new heart and right spirit." Then I went and kneeled down by my "trundle bed" and said, "Our Father which art in heaven," and realized sweetly that He was my reconciled Father.

He finally had peace with God. Yet, it was not long after that he had doubts. From that time until he was twenty, he felt like he was "locked up in the castle of Giant Despair, and could not find the key of faith." He felt like "a hungry child feeding on sawdust and shavings."

William felt far away from God. But then on August 28, at the age of twenty, William was restored in that relationship. At Panther Gap Camp Meeting he trusted in Christ again. Taylor, like many who come to know Christ, went through a period of doubt and needed the assurance that he was right with God. Before that camp meeting was through, he went at once to the streets to share his faith and to "street preach," a practice that would become a mark of his ministry on the streets of San Francisco.

# A Vision and A Calling

Soon after William became a Christian, he had a dream preaching, and at the close of the service the pastor dismissed t a hymn. He abruptly stopped his singing, fixed his eyes on ' "William, God has a great work for you to do and if you will co and blood, turn neither to the right hand or to the left, but fo' the Holy Spirit, your wisdom will increase like a continua bucket." In his dream he saw an empty bucket with pure sparkling drops falling into it. He learned from his dream to never say, "I am not prepared." For he knew deep inside that he would be prepared for anything God would bring his way.

The next Sunday after his vision, the pastor dismissed the congregation with a hymn. While they were on their way out, he stopped his singing, looked at William and said, "William, will you please go out!"

> I grabbed my hat and cut for home, a distance of two miles. Striding over the hills like a racer, I was wondering what on earth I could have done that our preacher should order me out of the class meeting.

He hadn't done anything. When his father returned home, he told him that "Brother Enos addressed the class and said, 'I have had my eye on William Taylor for some time, and I am satisfied that God has a great work for him to do, and if you think as I do in regard to him, I will be glad to give him a license to exhort.'" The vote was unanimous. His father went to call him back in but he was nowhere to be found.

> I soon began to realize the call of the Spirit, to devote my life wholly to soul-saving. Nothing else appeared to be worth living for....Again the Lord instructed me in the night seasons. In my sleep an invisible person who seemed to be close to me, talked most kindly and sweetly to my spirit, reminding me of the command of Jesus, "that they should not depart from Jerusalem, but wait for the promise of the Father...you shall receive power after that the Holy Ghost is come upon you."

With that, William Taylor's ministry had begun.

# Chapter Two

## Early Ministry as a Circuit Rider

In the early days of the Methodist revival movement, pastors would travel on horseback to their destinations to teach people in homes. John Wesley, the founder of the Methodist Church, kept a daily appointment of preaching to miners at five every morning. It was Wesley's desire to go where the people were, and would travel on horseback to get there. There was vast territory of North America that needed to be covered by a small number of pastors, which led to this circuit riding system of getting to people.

William, at the age of 21, was appointed to his first circuit of churches. He was appointed under the ministry of Thomas H. Busey. Busey was Taylor's early mentor, and described by Taylor as a man who was patient, kind, and a loving father to him. Since Busey was absent for a few weeks, Taylor took his place preaching. The Franklin Circuit was a four-week, seventy-five mile tour. He carried his Bible, hymnbook, and a copy of Clarke's Theology.

Before his appointment to the Franklin Circuit, he was asked to preach a round on the Lexington Circuit. This happened to be Taylor's native county as well as his home church. He was used to being taught, but was not used to being the teacher. This experience proved to be great preparation for his first circuit, for he learned a valuable lesson. He said that he "became as giddy-headed as a fresh sailor boy at the masthead and as blind as a bat on facing the sun." But he closed his eyes and prayed, learning that God would fill his mouth with the words to say. He learned the truth of the verse, "...do not worry beforehand about what to say. Just say whatever is given to you at the time, for it is not you speaking, but the Holy Spirit."

## Tasting Failure

On October 1, 1842, Taylor left home for the first time to preach. The first night on the circuit he stayed at the house of Esquire Jones, who lived near Cowpasture River. The next morning the 'squire escorted the young preacher to the church that met in a home nearby. Taylor later said of his preaching that he was never a flat failure in all his life, but the first day he preached he came close. Early on in his ministry he was very hard on himself, but found out later that those who were impacted by him had a much higher impression of him than he had. One man said, "He is muscular, and bony, tall and slender, with an immense pair of shoulders...he is awfully earnest, and preaches with power."

Taylor moved on to Crabbottom and North Folk, and then crossed the mountains to Franklin where he was introduced for the first time to his colleague, Thomas Busey. Busey had been to Crabbottom after William had left and brought back the report from one brother that "He'll do; he is very young and inexperienced, but he's got the stuff in him and will do us good service."

William accompanied Busey to Back Creek, and arranged to spend the night at his Grandfather's house. His grandpa said, "If Will Taylor comes here pretending to preach I will send him home to his mother." His grandfather, like his dad, was a mechanical genius. He made many of the tools on his farm with his own hands. While he spoke with his Aunt and Uncle, William noticed his grandfather taking the furthest seat away from him. Yet Taylor knew how to communicate with him.

"Grandfather, how is your mill working now?" Taylor announced across the room.

"Like a charm; she never did better work than she is doing now." He continued by asking him questions about hunting and trapping, and with each successive question, Will was able to draw his grandfather closer to him. Later he was asked to conduct family worship in their home, and his grandfather began seeing his need for Christ in his own life.

Before Taylor left, his grandfather told him to "preach in my house every time you come around." William felt sure that his grandfather started his relationship with God soon after.

The Conference year ended in February of 1843 and Taylor was able to go home to be with his family for a month. He had spent five months on the Franklin Circuit and was ready for a good visit. Then on April 1, he received a letter from his elder that said he had been appointed to the Baltimore Annual Conference, to minister with Rev. Zane Bland on the Deerfield Circuit.

# Organizing a Movement

The Deerfield Circuit included the mountain regions of Augusta, Rockbridge, Bath, and Pendleton Counties. They were all poor farming districts that did not have any towns. William found the people to be "a loving, plain, kind, and appreciative class of mountaineers." It was on the Deerfield that he led his first class meeting.

Like the circuit ministry, the class meetings were a mark of early Methodism. One biographer writes,

> (Wesley) had bound them together in a united whole, but he found a further step to be necessary. The people were widely scattered throughout London, and as such it was impossible for him to keep an oversight of their personal life. This gave birth to a new working Wesleyan unit, of which he says, "At length while we were thinking of quite another thing we struck upon a method for which we have cause to bless God ever since." He broke down his parent society into smaller working units known as classes.

John Wesley was a master organizer. Where other revival movements came and went, John organized this particular movement into a working ministry that still exists today. His first organizational plan was to bring the people together into societies. Then, as the societies grew, they were multiplied into classes. Soon, the classes were voluntarily multiplied into bands. Wesley's General Rules (for these societies) was written in 1743, and reads as a how-to for small groups.

Taylor used these groups in San Francisco and later in his church planting strategy in India. The home of a Mr. Joseph was the setting for Taylor's first class meeting.

"Now we will have a class meeting. But few of you know what sort of a meeting that is." Taylor went on to describe how they "did some lively singing, and I told a little of my own experience of the saving grace of God." Taylor spoke to each person individually to see how his or her relationship with God was. "The first one I tackled was a burly-looking fellow with reddish sandy whiskers, clad in homespun, home woven, and homemade woolen, dyed brown in ooze of walnut bark."

Taylor continued his conversation with the man. He shook hands with the man and asked, "How are you?"

"Very well, I thank you. How does it go with yourself?" the man asked back.

"First rate, thank the Lord! I am well, soul and body, and I am glad to make your acquaintance. Will you kindly give me your name?"

"Yes sir; my name is Radcliffe."

"You are a farmer, I presume?"

"Yes, sir; I own a little farm about a mile from here."

"Well stocked, I hope, and under good cultivation."

"Yes, sir; I have cattle, horses, pigs, and sheep and am putting a pretty large crop of corn. My wheat and rye last year were above the average for this country."

"And your family?"

"Yes sir; I have a wife and four children."

"All enjoying good health?"

"Yes sir; no reason to complain."

"Every gift is from our gracious God and Father. I am glad, Mr. Radcliffe, he thinks so much of you, and of your wife and children, as to bestow all these mercies on you. I hope you take off your hat to him sometimes and say, 'Thank you?'"

"Well sir; I am sorry to say I forgot that."

"What a pity! When we receive a gift from anybody, we always have the good manners that mother taught us, to say, 'Thank you;' and yet you say for all God's gifts you have never said, 'Thank you.'"

"I am very sorry that I have been so forgetful, but I hope from this day I will think more of these things and learn to say 'Thank you' to God."

The purpose of the class meetings was to do what the regular worship service could not—share in each other's personal lives. William led the class in holding each participant accountable

# Log Roller or Holy Roller?

On his stop at Red Holes, Taylor hitched his horse and headed up the hill to the country chapel where he found two old ladies. As he entered, they told him that they did not expect the preachers to be in since they had to travel two hundred miles from conference. They had not been expecting the young preacher to be there so soon when he introduced himself, saying that he was one of them.

"All our men are engaged at a logrolling a quarter of a mile west of here. Some of the women are helping to prepare the supper for the logrollers, and the rest are at home."

"Well, sisters, I can't come here for nothing." He proceeded to tell them that they needed to announce to the other women that he would be preaching that night, and he would go round up the men.

Taylor rode up to the edge of the clearing, hitched his horse, and hiked up to where the others were. Without saying a word, he picked up a handspike, and began to level the logs wherever he wanted them to land. The other loggers began to eye him, wondering who he might be. He announced to the crowd that had gathered some distance from him, "The young preacher sent to your circuit by the bishop will preach in the chapel tonight. Get through your supper as quickly as you can and all come and hear the young preacher."

"Are you sure the preacher has come?" they asked.

"O, yes, indeed; there is no doubt on that subject."

"Wonder if a great logroller like you can be the preacher?"

"Come and see."

Someone in the crowd of men said, "If he is as good in the use of the Bible as he is of the handspike he'll do."

Another commented, "He don't belong to your Miss Nancy, soft-handed, kid-gloved gentry." They all agreed that they would hear the preacher that night. Every time Taylor went to Red Holes, they would crowd the house and many came to know Christ through those meetings.

# Queen Anne

One quick comment must be made about his ministry on the Fincastle Circuit. He had many people come to know the Lord on this tour, but one who would stick with him for the rest of his life. Annie Kimberlin came to know two special men during this year, Jesus and William. It was understood by the young preachers that they must have served the church for four years before they could get married. Not much more is said about his relationship with Annie until his ministry in Georgetown.

## Sweet Springs Circuit

One year Taylor was appointed to the dreaded Sweet Springs Circuit. Many saw the circuit as a hopeless undertaking, yet Will liked nothing less than a challenge. His name was read in connection with Sweet Springs at the conference.

The only chapel he found on the circuit was at Gap Hills. Sweet Springs, the "town," had only three Christians in the whole valley. One was a Roman Catholic, and the other two were women belonging to the Methodist Church. The rest of those in the valley were not connected with any church. The practice on many of the circuits was to use homes to house the local worshipers. On the whole circuit there were not any more than thirty to forty people who were interested in what William had to offer.

Then, events began to turn for the better on one of his stops. He was making his way up to Jake Weekline's house on a Wednesday night to find two rooms of the house overflowing with people. They were there to hear the young preacher. It was announced the Sunday before that he would be there, and after seeing the interest, he announced that he would keep an appointment with them to come every other Sunday as well.

The next Sunday arrived, and Will found the house so full that they made their way out to a field underneath the shade of a sugar maple tree. Two weeks later the group grew even larger and he decided to hold a service every morning and evening for a week. He told the Weeklines, "God is going to give us an ingathering of souls, and I will organize here the biggest class on the circuit and appoint Joe Carson the class leader for it."

Others who had heard his announcement began to laugh. Joe was very bitter towards Christians and was known as the worst swearer in the valley.

The week long "revival" commenced and many came to know what it meant to have their sins forgiven. All throughout the week, people were seeking salvation, including Joe:

> Looking over my audience, I saw, to my agreeable surprise, Joe Carson and his wife. They had come ten miles on horseback that morning to attend my meetings; so I thanked God, and in my heart prayed earnestly for them. After preaching there in the open air that forenoon I invited seekers to come forward for instruction and the prayers of those who knew God, and kneel

at a row of benches set for the purpose. About a dozen came promptly, and among them was Mrs. Carson. Joe saw her down, and sprang to his feet and ran to the woods like a wounded deer. He ran about one hundred yards and fell prostrate on the ground.

Joe Carson presented himself to William as a seeker of salvation later that day, and testified to him that Jesus saved him from his sins. That year Joe Carson proved to the young preacher that he was an able leader, so William appointed him as the leader of the class meeting that met at the Weekline's. One hundred people were added to Sweet Springs that year, and what was known as uncharted territory before William arrived, was now a fully organized circuit.

# From Circuit to Station

After the Conference in March of 1846, William was appointed to the Georgetown Station. Just like a soldier being stationed in one place, William was stationed in his first city for the coming year. And with the appointment came some advice.

"Brother William, I have come to have a friendly, confidential talk with you. You know how I loved your parents, and I must say I feel a great interest in you for their sake as well as for your own. I congratulate you on receiving one of the best appointments for a young man in the gift of the Conference. I have some knowledge of the Georgetown people. They are an intelligent, liberal, devoted people—devoted to God and to their Church; but associated as they are with Washington City, they are a very fashionable people, more fashionable than the good people of Baltimore. I want you to make a good impression on Georgetown at the start and gain a standing among the higher classes. A part of my business is to take you to Brother Jarrett's tailor shop and give your measure for a new suit of clothes. Brother Jarrett will give you a splendid fit in the latest style, so that you can appear respectably before a Georgetown audience."

"Why, my brother, I have a new suit of clothes from top to toe, including overcoat and boots," Taylor responded.

"O, yes, I see that, but your coats are too short in the waist, and there is nothing in your whole rig that is up to the standard of fashion at the capital."

"They were in fashion where I came from," said Taylor, "and I am not responsible for the changes of fashion that the city folks are making continually," Taylor replied. "I am much obliged, my dear brother, for your kind advice, but I am, the

Lord willing, going to Georgetown in my new mountain suit, and if the good people there don't like the cut of it they can look in the opposite direction."

Taylor knew that his brother was sincere and that he did not mean him any harm. He only wanted the best for William. William made one hundred dollars every year through the Conference, and could not see putting his hard earned money into outward appearances. Commenting later, William said, "I did not wish to predicate my standing in my new station on my outward adornment so much as by inward endowment and the favor with the people which the Lord might be pleased to give me."

When he made his appearance at Georgetown, he never tried to look, act, or preach any differently. He would not sugarcoat the truth of God in order to adapt it to whatever people wanted to hear, but what they *needed* to hear.

Soon after he arrived in that great city, he began to sense a call to preach in the streets. He decided to preach on Sunday afternoons in the Georgetown Market. On a Sunday afternoon in April of 1846, he began by singing loudly and drew up a crowd. His newly formed congregation was orderly and well behaved, and always paid attention to what he was saying. This would not be the last of his appointments preaching outside the four walls of the church.

# Engagement

Taylor's presiding elder was the Rev. T.B. Sargent. At one of his camp meetings, William requested a confidential interview.

"Brother Sargent, I have for a year and a half been engaged to be married to Miss Annie Kimberlin, on Fincastle Circuit. It was understood that we would not be married until I serve the Church four years as a single man. I have already traveled four years, including six months under the presiding elder before I joined the Conference. If I shall be married this fall I will finish my fourth Conference year on a single man's allowance and support my wife in the meantime from my own pocket, so that practically I will have served as a single man four years from the time of joining the Conference."

After asking Sargent's advice, Taylor was given permission to take a few weeks absence so that he could get married in the fall. In October of 1846, he was married by a good friend at the home of Annie's grandmother, on a bluff overlooking the James River in Botetourt County, Virginia. Four years separated husband and wife, but William later commented that "she looked much younger and I much older than we really were." When walking the avenues of Washington the remark was often dropped by passing observers, "There goes that beautiful young lady and her father."

# Freeing Slaves

Taylor married into an undivided estate in which there were close to a dozen slaves. At the Conference of 1847, he announced to those present that as soon as her youngest sister was of age or married, they would free every one of the slaves. In reply the bishop said, "If F.A. Harding had made a manly speech of that sort at the Conference of 1844 it might have prevented a split that ripped our Church in two. We want no better pledge, Brother Taylor, than what you have just given." Four years after his announcement the youngest heir was married, and on the night of her marriage a deed was signed to free the remaining slaves. Taylor personally gave them one thousand dollars in gold and his father got them aboard a ship bound for Liberia.

# The Call to California

In 1848, the General Conference made provision for the founding of a church in California. They wanted to send two able pastors for the work. There was much attention being drawn to that area due to the discovery of gold. Bishop Waugh told Taylor that the venture would require "men of great physical force and courage, men of pure hearts and clean hands, and clear exponents of Methodism in doctrine, experience, and practical life." The first man that was appointed was Rev. Isaac Owen of the Indiana Conference. Owen began the work for the Methodist Church in Sacramento. Indiana, up until the time of expansion to the California region, was known as the "west." Since Owen was from the "west," they wanted a man from the "east" to go as well.

The Bishop asked, "From what I have learned and seen of you I think you are the man for that difficult work, and I have called you in to inquire if you will accept the appointment?"

"I had not thought of such a possibility, and had no thought of offering myself for that or any other specific work," Taylor later wrote. "But I was called to preach the Gospel by the Holy Spirit under the old commission, 'Go ye into all the world and preach the Gospel to every creature,' and I suppose that includes California…. It is not for me to say I am the man suitable for California, but leaving myself entirely at His disposal, giving you wisdom to express His will concerning me, I will cheerfully accept your decision and abide by it."

"Go home and consult your wife about it, and let me know by next Wednesday at my house." That is what William did. The first words to his wife when she met him at the door were, "Bishop Waugh wants to send us as missionaries to California. What do you think of that?" She didn't answer him, but ran straight upstairs to her bedroom.

Confused, William made his way into the house and sat down. No sooner had he sat down that Anne came running back down the stairs smiling, saying, "Yes, I'll go with you to California."

"How did you settle the question so quickly?" William asked.

"I went upstairs and kneeled down and said, 'Lord, Bishop Waugh wants to send us to California. Thou knowest, Lord, that I don't want to go, and can see no possible way of getting there; but all things are possible with thee, and if it is thy will to send us to California, give me the desire to go.' In a second or two he filled and thrilled my whole being with a desire to go to California." The question was settled and they began to prepare for their trip to the west.

# Chapter Three

## How the West Was *Really* Won

There were three ways to go west at that time. Many went through the plains, two thousand miles west of the Missouri River on a trail blazed by General Fremont. Another way was to go by steamboat up the Chagres River, across the Isthmus of Panama and then by riding mule the rest of the way or walking on foot. The third route was by way of sailing vessels around Cape Horn. Taylor was able to secure passage on the ship called the Andalusia. She was a Baltimore clipper that was superior to the other ships in his day. A family had backed out of first class that left the opening for William and Anne. On June 3, 1849, their third child, Oceana was born off Cape Horn. She lived only fourteen months and, as her father put it, "left us for the city of the great King."

Their only stop on the voyage was at Valparaiso, where they spent the Sunday with a missionary from the Presbyterian Board. William preached for him that Sunday morning. It was also in Valparaiso that they heard the first news of their destination.

One man told him that Governor Mason of California had been removed from office by the mob. Another said that the only known preacher in the city was killed by the miners, packed in a barrel and marked "beef." Others reported that anarchy ruled throughout the region. Yet he got word from other voyagers that the above stories were not true, so Taylor ignored the news as an attempt by

Satan to terrify them through his lies. What was true, however, is that men felt God did not hold them accountable for the things they did west of the Mississippi.

The Taylors reached their destination in September of 1849. They anchored in the harbor of San Francisco one hundred and fifty-five days after setting sail from Baltimore.

San Francisco was still a city of tents. When they landed, he asked a brother who boarded the ship whether there were any other Christian Churches in California. He told them that they had one preacher, but since preaching didn't pay, he went to gambling.

He ascended the hill above Clark's Point with Captain Wilson and got their first view of the city. There was not a brick house in the whole city. There were some wooden structures, but most were tents. Taylor began asking whether there were any Methodists in the city. He was able to find one, and he introduced William to Rev. O.C. Wheeler, a Baptist minister who asked Taylor to preach, which he did that next Sunday.

On October 8, a Methodist Episcopal Church was shipped from Oregon and set up on Powell Street lot. He preached what was the first Protestant sermon in Alameda County on the twenty-first of that month. He felt a burden, however, on the missionary society that sent him. He hoped that "by the labor of a few weeks I can live without another draft on the funds of the society. Oh, my Master, help me in my work of avoiding expense to the missionary board." He never wanted to be a burden to anyone, which is why he would establish himself as a self-supporting missionary then and later in Africa.

A story is told in *The Beginnings of San Francisco* about the building of the Taylor home: "Landing in San Francisco in September, 1849, after a long trip around Cape Horn, he could find no shelter for his wife…. Brother Taylor did go to the redwoods, accompanied by a good brother who volunteered to help him, and after some weeks of arduous and unaccustomed labor, succeeded in getting his lumber and building his house on a lot another brother helped him to buy."

William was able to gather a group of Methodists in his twenty-four by thirty-six foot chapel. On December 3, 1849, Taylor announced to his congregation that he would be going out to the Plaza in San Francisco to preach. This was a dangerous adventure, for the gamblers were a very influential and powerful group of men:

> The Plaza was the public square, but the lair of gamblers was so numerous and commanded so much influence that in that day they were above the law. Men were shot, carried out, and buried

like dogs with no arrests. At the hour appointed, in company with his equally heroic young wife, he walked to the Plaza, a few of his people following, and mounted a carpenter's work bench in front of a large saloon. With a voice that could be heard by nearly half the city he opened the battle with the martial music of the Royal Proclamation.... Hundreds of excited men came running from every direction, the gambling houses emptied, the crowds surrounded him. They came to arrest him, but instead, he arrested them.... He captured their minds and their hearts. Perfect order was observed; profound attention given. That night at the altar in the chapel men presented themselves as seekers of salvation. He started the first revival in California.

Taylor preached to a variety of crowds. He wrote *Seven Years Street Preaching in San Francisco* to detail his work there. In this book he gave his reason for taking the gospel to the streets: "There are hundreds of men in the mines who have heard no preaching in California except what they have heard on the Plaza in this city." Like Wesley, who woke up at four every morning to preach to the miners at five, Taylor wanted to bring God's Word to those on the streets as well.

The book not only gives an account of what he did, but also gives some suggestions as to how to preach in the streets. As he did in class as a youngster, Taylor used humor in his preaching. At many times, he found some who would try to break up the crowd by being loud and obnoxious. On one Sunday, one man "thinking to have a little sport," tried to ride through the crowd on his donkey. The donkey would not pass through, and so in order to bring the people back into focus on God's Word, Taylor proclaimed:

"See there, that animal, like Balaam's of the same kind, has more respect for the worship of God than his master, who only lacks the ears of being the greater ass of the two."

On another occasion Taylor appealed to the crowd's higher morals. One man who was trying to create a disturbance, was surprised by Taylor's line of questioning:

"See here, my friend, when did you arrive here?" asked Taylor.

"I came from the old country, about six years ago."

"But I want to know when you came to California?"

"O, a good while ago."

"How many days since?"

The man hesitated and looked for an opening in the crowd so that he could escape. He then replied, "About two weeks ago, sir."

"I knew by your conduct that you had recently arrived, and had not learned how to behave yourself here yet. You seem to imagine that we were all a set of heathen here in California, and that you could 'cut up,' and do as you please. Now as you are a stranger in these parts, I will inform you that the order of the day in California is for all classes of society to respect the preaching of the Gospel, and never to disturb a preacher in the discharge of his duty, and the fellow that dare persist in such an outrage may expect that even the gamblers will 'give him a licking.'"

## Whisky Barrel Pulpit

On one occasion, Taylor used a turned over whisky barrel as a pulpit. Standing on his "pulpit," he introduced his subject:

> Gentlemen, I have for my pulpit today, as you see, a barrel of whiskey. I presume this is the first time this barrel has ever been appropriated to a useful purpose. The 'critter' contained in it will do me no harm while I keep it under my feet. And let me say now to you all, to sailors and to landsmen, never let the 'critter' get above your feet. Keep it *under your feet,* and you have nothing to fear from it.

Taylor kept a busy Sunday schedule: He led class at 9a.m., preached on the Long Wharf at 10a.m. He preached in the Bethel (which was a structure he built to house sailors) at 11a.m. and at the State Marine Hospital at 2:30. On some mornings, he distributed tracts to 150 patients, allowing them to read the plan of salvation, possibly for the first time. He was back on the Plaza at 4:00 and the Bethel once again at 7:00. He admitted that it might be "much for one man to do, but the Lord gives me strength to do it, without inconvenience or injury to myself." A usual Sunday crowd at the Plaza would consist of at least 1,000 hearers.

He would preach at a number of funerals as well, many who died from drinking. Sometimes Taylor was the only "family" these people had, as well as the only person who showed up at their funerals. His church may have been located on a hill, but his congregation was the city of San Francisco.

He never allowed a collection to be taken up for his benefit while he was out in the streets. "My reason is, that in the streets, I proclaim a free gospel." He did collect money for the building of the Bethel, however. The Bethel was a resting stop for sailors. When they did not have a place to stay, Taylor wanted to erect a building that would meet their needs physically. Taylor may have preached, feeding the flocks spiritually, but he also took care of their physical needs as well.

# Class Meetings

From the streets he would announce to the group that they could meet in their "church on the hill" for more teaching. He wrote in his journal that on Sunday, February 3rd, 1850, ninety people came. Most were from many parts of the world and had been touched by the ministry of the Methodists. They all "told the same story of redemption through the blood of Jesus, even the forgiveness of their sins."

The effects of his ministry in California were far reaching. Many of those who heard William's preaching had stories like this sailor's to tell:

> I became a sailor and got very wicked. But soon after I came to California, in the early part of 1850, I heard Brother Taylor singing on the Plaza one Sunday afternoon, and I went up and listened to what he had to say. The truth took hold of my heart, and that week God converted my soul. I am happy to find so many friends here in California, lovers of Jesus. I believe, verily, that God will fetch me through.

Taylor also had an effect on "business" in the area. Taylor tells a story in *Seven Years Street Preaching* of when one man tried to get the attention of the audience. Screaming at the top of his lungs, he was calling Taylor an impostor who was only out for their money. Instead of William turning the tide through humor or quick thinking, one man yelled out, "Stop stranger, what is your business here in the city?"

Answering only when hard pressed by the crowd, the man replied, "Why, sir, I am a gambler, and I did a first-rate business, and made money here, 'til these preachers came to the city. But this fellow is hallooing at the people here every Sunday, and has broken up my business. I can't get a decent living." Through his preaching, William Taylor broke up the man's business, and never saw the gambler again.

# Street Preacher to Hospital Helper

William's desire was not only to preach to the people, but to minister to them in practical ways as well. He made a regular visit to the City Hospital, which was half-jokingly called the depot of death. Sometimes a patient would be asked to lay in between two dead men. The stench was so strong that many would get sick at the sight of all the death around them. Taylor's usual practice of visitation included talking with as many patients as he could. He would ask them what their condition was, whether they had any needs both physically and spiritually, and would record messages for them to be sent home to their families.

The preacher even turned doctor at times. He would dress blisters, help the patients turn over or get up, give them something to drink, or even bring some of Mrs. Taylor's homemade bread. He would counsel some and sing with others. Many would be confronted with the claims of Christ for the first time and would come to know him as a result of Taylor's work in the hospital.

Taylor's book on street preaching also records "triumphant death scenes," where a number of cases were recorded of patients coming to know Christ. But there were others as well who would not turn to Jesus.

"I remember after pleading with a dying man to give his heart to God he said, 'O, it's not worth while now; I'm getting better; I'll soon be well. I feel no pain at all, and nothing ails me now but want of breath. I can't breathe easy; but I'll soon be relieved.' Poor man! I could then hear distinctly the death-rattle in his throat, and yet he would not believe there was any danger." In a few hours he was dead. There were victories as well as defeats, and Taylor had to learn to live with them all.

# Among the Miners

The promise was that anyone who made the trip to the gold mines could become rich. But not all the miners were successful. Each of them held out hope, however. No matter what their past was in going for the gold, each of them held out a glimmer of hope that the next dig would bring the dollars. They lived on hope, but died in despair.

Sundays were far from a day of rest. It was a day for trading, recreation, and business meetings in order to plan for the next week. It was the day for the miners to get their blacksmith work done. Mining districts were set up so that laws could be passed by majority rule. It was also a day for drinking as well.

Taylor traveled among the mines and was hard-pressed to find any other Christians. In one town he found one who the town hailed as a good Christian man. Taylor went to visit him and his family only to find that he couldn't practice his ministry because he did his blacksmithing on Sundays. That was the only way he could feed his family.

In another area he was able to get a large crowd together under a large pine tree. When the evening came around, he had hoped for an even larger crowd, but found that they were all too drunk to make it to the outside service. His appointments among the miners were disappointing to him. There were times when people would crowd around him on the streets, and other times where he could hardly gather a small family of people.

# The Great Fire

On Saturday May 3, 1851, a fire broke out that ravaged the city and destroyed an estimated twelve to twenty million dollars of property and possessions. Many of the streets were wooden, and on each side were wooden sewers. Instead of allowing water to flow freely through its tunnels, the sewers acted as a flue that brought the destructive flames through the city. In the midst of the confusion and crying, William Taylor sang out "one of Zion's sweetest songs." Through his singing he was able to bring together thousands of people, and this occasion was not unlike the rest. A confused mob became a comforted crowd as Taylor sang and announced his text: "Except the Lord build the house, they labor in vain that build it. Except the Lord keep the city, the watchman waketh but in vain."

The soldier marched for seven years on the streets of San Francisco, drawing the masses to the Savior. In those seven years, he preached six hundred sermons to thousands of people. It was his desire to bring church to those who would not set foot in a church of their own.

William Taylor is marked as California Taylor. A panel of famous mural paintings hung in the reference room of the old San Francisco Public Library and is now located at the San Francisco Arts Commission. This panel commemorates the pioneer spirit of early America. It shows a group of pioneers leaving the east. Marching in the center of that group is William Taylor, with an open Bible in his hand. California crowned him as the embodiment of the moral forces of which the state was proud.

He was California Taylor to those in the West, but he would become much more in a very short time.

# Chapter Four

## Igniting Revival

Looking out over the waters of the Atlantic, William's mind drifted to the memories of his daughter Oceana and his son Willie, who both had gone to be with the Lord, each too young to die. His thoughts wandered from the wounds of death to the financial problems left in San Francisco. In 1856, before helping to ignite the flames of revival in the East, another fire had swept through the streets, destroying a home and the the Bethel built for the sailors. This left him with a bill that he wanted to pay through the sale of his book. The Taylors were on their way to New York on a ship owned by the Pacific Mail Steamship Company, in order to "labor as an evangelist, and to print and circulate (his) first book, *Seven Years Street Preaching in San Francisco.*"

They arrived in New York, with his first matter of business to publish his work. His excitement was laid aside when the Taylors lost their third child, Osman, who was only two years old.

## Evangelist

During the years of 1857-62, Taylor toured the Midwest, New England, and Canada. It was in '57 that the Great Revival spread. He was one of the torchbearers of the flames of that revival. One of Taylor's first engagements was to hold services in 1857 in Monument Street Church in Baltimore. He preached in Eutaw and Charles Street churches, where the last church was the "only pewed church" south of the Mason-Dixon line. Ben Brook was the pastor of this church composed mostly of businessmen and bankers. The church was twelve years old, and in that time had never held revival services. Ben wanted William to help him in conducting a series of services, but Taylor did not feel comfortable until the leading members could agree on the idea. The trustees could not agree to open the church while they were so busy during the evenings conducting business. Ben sat down in disappointment, but then rose, trembling with emotion, and gave the church leaders an ultimatum.

"I have been working here for over a year, and have seen but little success in soul saving. You are all very kind to me; there is no better station in the city, but I cannot stand this sort of work any longer. I must see something done or quit. Brother Taylor is with us and can help us. He cannot be with us in the fall, the usual time for revivals; so my feeling is that if you won't concur in this proposal I shall have to put on my hat and bid you good-bye."

The room grew silent. Taylor leaned over to Brook, whispering that he did not agree to work under these circumstances. But the pastor, obviously impassioned for the people of that city, convinced Taylor otherwise. Their secret discussion was broken up by the voice of one of the leaders.

"Well Brother Brook, we have expressed our minds plainly, and have not changed our view of the case; but if you and Brother Taylor are willing to face the failure and disgrace of an abortive attempt, then go ahead; we will not stand in your way."

Taylor and Brook decided on how they would go about their work. They were going to hold services in the main sanctuary, instead of the basement where revival services had been held before. They held meetings at 11a.m. every day of the week, and used the rest of the day to visit. They examined everyone personally to see whether their profession of faith was true, and kept records of their names and addresses for further follow-up. Brook would preach the regular services during the week, and Taylor preached the other appointments.

During each of the weekday services, they had over fifty people attend. Those who were Christians were encouraged to bring friends. News began to spread throughout the city regarding the change that God was bringing in people's lives. Proof of this fact came from the voice of one of the church's leading members, Major Dryden. Up to this point his voice was never heard in prayer, but it was a different story on this occasion.

"O, Lord, twelve years ago we built this house," Dryden prayed. "We poured out our money freely and constructed this beautiful edifice. These fine pews have been sepulchers to the dead, and these fine cushions the habiliments of our graves. We have had good preaching, but we awoke not. O, Lord, thou knowest how helpless and hopeless was our deplorable state. But during these meetings, blessed be thy holy name, the voice of the Son of God has awakened the dead, and they have come forth a great army, and are on the march for the conquest of souls for thee. Now we are glad that we put our money into this beautiful building, and that at last, thou hast accepted this our offering, and we will trust thee henceforth to make this the house of thine abode, for Christ's sake. Amen!"

As Taylor and Brook preached, and as the people reached out to their neighbors, the Charles Street Church added over two hundred new Christians to her membership. From Baltimore, Taylor preached at twelve camp meetings in New Jersey, Delaware, and Maryland. He preached in many cities, once again taking the good news to the streets, even if it was against the city's laws. His courage set other pastors in those cities to preaching in the streets, many of whom were outside of Methodist circles.

## Meetings in the Midwest

Through the summer of 1858 to 1860, Taylor preached six days out of the week in many of the cities and towns of Ohio, Indiana, and Illinois. The method for this Methodist was to preach, and invite "seekers of pardon or purity to come to the altar." From there he instructed them and prayed for them. With others in these churches, he would listen to the testimonies of the people who came forward, which lasted until after 9p.m. On Monday nights he would give talks on what God was doing in California, which many came to enjoy.

Youth ministry was not beyond the scope of Taylor's ministry. On Sunday afternoons, Taylor preached to the children who crowded the church, with many of them coming to know the Lord as well. Looking out over the crowd of two hundred children, Taylor recalled how these children, once known as "wharf rats," came to be seated in his Wesley Church children's meeting.

## Wharf Rats

Samuel Clayton was a pastor, but had not been appointed to any church. He was sent to the neglected classes in the city as a missionary. He encouraged parents to send their children to a room he had rented out for church. The first Sunday was a disaster. There was complete disorder. The children were in the practice of pulling each other's hair, and pricking each other with pins. Clayton was at the end of his rope. He closed his eyes to pray. To his amazement the voices of the children were silent. Clayton continued his prayer, opened his eyes, only to find an empty room. Bare-footed, the children were able to slip out without him noticing.

Clayton did not let up. He visited many of them during the week, and invited them for a second Sunday. They all came, with all the same behavior and loudness as before. Then he began to sing a "quick-time tune to easy words," and they became quiet. He dismissed them, and later that week, as he was walking along the bank of the Ohio River, he heard some singing in the background.

Off in the distance, he could see a group of children singing under the cover of an upturned boat. As he walked closer, he recognized the song he had taught them the Sunday before. He thought inwardly, "Now, my lads, I've got you. I have already won you by sacred song, and will hold you and lead you to God." Taylor's camp meeting was filled with well-dressed, well-behaved children, all of whom were a testimony to the work of Samuel Clayton.

In his own autobiography, Taylor detailed many stories of other people who have worked in the cause for Christ, Clayton being one of many.

# Canada

William was able to work with his wife, Anne, and their two little boys. The family stayed in the home of a Canadian regiment colonel. The possibility of war with the United States was in the air, and Taylor accompanied the colonel into the city. As they walked the streets the men wanted to know, "What's the order of the day?"

"The first thing is for you to be introduced to my good brother here, California Taylor. He is a true native-born American, the author of some very interesting books." The colonel took to the streets during the day to recruit soldiers, but many did not want to enlist, either because they thought war with the United States was not going to happen, or because they were afraid that war was immanent. Taylor's work was hindered for a while because of the excitement about the war. He spent the spring of 1861 to the spring of '62 preaching in Upper and Lower Canada. He would preach six days out of the week and held nine camp meetings that year. He reported that the work, "under the blessing of Providence reached thousands of souls."

J.W. Clinton, recalling one of those camp meetings, reported that the camp, in a grove north of St. George, was a tremendous success.

This was a remarkable camp meeting, and Father Taylor was then at his prime.… I call to mind an anecdote he related about a father at Terre Haute, Indiana, who descended by sliding down a rope into a well to save his daughter Lizzie, who had fallen in. He saved his daughter, but so ruined his hands that they were of no use to him in his employment ever after. This father he compared to Jesus coming down to save us, and with such telling effect that the vast assemblage was moved to tears. At that camp meeting over one hundred were converted, and about eighty were baptized at its close, selecting as they chose all three modes, sprinkling, pouring, and immersion.

Another man, John Clark Ridpath, remembered Taylor's preaching when he was a student at Indiana Asbury (now De Pauw) University. He recalled Taylor's "directness of speech which is, perhaps, the secret of his influence in the religious society of our time."

He felt that his ability was a natural gift. "Bishop Taylor learned to be direct. Many others have learned the lesson from him. A large part of the successful evangelism of the age has sprung from him and from his method," Ridpath said.

In the winter of 1862, Taylor preached in Great St. James Wesleyan Church in Montreal. Many of the people in those services were men in the armed services. British soldiers made up a number of the men in that large hall in the city. Taylor delivered a series of sermons on abstaining from alcohol, and many came forward to write their names in a book he used for them to sign the pledge. One soldier came up, and wanted to do just that. He was not a Christian yet, and told Taylor that he did not even know how to pray to God. The soldier wanted Taylor to write him a prayer, so that he could repeat it and then God might hear him and save him. Taylor said in reply, "My dear brother, there are some little prayers recorded in the New Testament which will suit you better than any I can write for you. The prayer of blind Bartimeus is a good one. 'Jesus, thou Son of David, have mercy on me a sinner.'" The man agreed to pray that prayer, telling Taylor that he had duty in the barracks that night, and if he were spared, would pray that prayer.

Alarmed, Taylor replied, "Don't wait until tomorrow night. You may be dead before that time. You can pray now, or in the barracks tonight you may kneel down by your bunk and surrender to God and receive Christ. He can save you in the barracks just as well as in Great St. James Church."

The next night William saw his friend in the audience. When he invited seekers to the altar, the soldier marched down the aisle. Reaching Taylor he commented, "I have not come to seek the Lord tonight; I have come to testify. You said the Lord Jesus would save me last night in the barracks if I would call upon him. So I kneeled down by my bunk, and the soldiers began to swear at me, saying 'Here is a fellow on his knees,' and they pelted me with their old boots and shoes and whatever they could get a hold of. But I paid no attention to them. I kept on crying, 'God be merciful to me a sinner.'

He continued, "I felt worse and worse, until finally I surrendered to God and received Christ, and the Holy Spirit notified me of my pardon, just as you said he would. I was acquitted at the bar of justice, and he wrought in me a marvelous change, which is indescribable. I lay in my bunk and praised God all the rest of the night, and all this day I have been walking the streets of Montreal praising God for this great salvation."

The Great Revival swept through the states and Canada that year, bringing people to Christ one-by-one.

# Chapter Five

# Ireland and England

While William was preaching in Peterboro, Canada, he stayed in the house of Dr. James Brown, who spent a number of years ministering in Australia. He told Taylor of the rise of that great island, and attempted to convince him that he needed to go work there. Brown felt that the time was ripe for an evangelist such as Taylor, and hoped Taylor would take him up on his offer.

The only convincing William needed, was from God. So he went out into the forest, knelt down in the snow, and asked whether God wanted him to go to Australia. Christ convinced him that Australia was his next move, but before jumping onto the steamship Kangaroo, he spent some time in California with his family. On May 1, 1862, Taylor was a first-class passenger on his way to another great adventure. His voyage did not take him straight to Australia. He first landed on the foggy coast of Ireland, where he labored there as well as in England.

## Preaching to a Kangaroo

For the past few years, William had been used to preaching a few times on Sundays, and would have felt uncomfortable if he did not preach at least once on a Sunday. Being used to having the captain ask whether he wanted to preach, this time he had to approach the leader of the ship. The captain thought it a good idea, and told him that he would have the officer of the deck make an announcement to the passengers. When time came to preach, William found no one. He went to the officer and asked whether any arrangements had been made. The man replied that he had not been given any direction to make such an announcement, and both men found the captain fast asleep in his room. The two Sundays of the voyage were met with promises that the captain would make sure a service would be held, but on each, he failed to follow through.

Once he landed, Taylor was able to join a Wesleyan Conference in session in Camborne, Cornwall. He visited and preached in many of the same places that John Wesley had preached in. Over a period of four months, he worked in different cities, holding week long services in places like Dublin and Belfast. During his trip to Armagh, he sat around the dinner table and discussed the pros and cons of the civil war in, what one man called, the "dis-United States." The London Times did not do much to lift the fog of false information, so Taylor decided to write another book entitled, *The Cause and Probable Results of the Civil War in America—Fact for the People of Great Britain.* So in 1863, his work was published in London and eleven thousand copies were distributed. The pamphlet was used by some as textbooks when giving lectures in the principal centers of England, and helped many in England understand what was really going on within the walls of the young nation.

# Traveling with a Baptist in Palestine

After spending another seven months in England and Ireland, William had to make good on his promise to sail to the south. He wanted to go by way of Palestine, so that he could see the area in which his Lord lived. But while he was still in London, a young Baptist pastor who had heard William lecture in St. James Hall, pressed Taylor to take him on his journey. At first he declined, but after more encouragement from his mom, Taylor decided to take him. So in 1863, Taylor and his new friend Jimmy, headed for Paris.

They spent a week looking at the sights of Paris, and then took a steamer to Syria. There in the city of Beirut, they met a man who wrote a history of Palestine, Dr. Thomson. He made a map of places to see while they were in the Holy Land. The next day, they set out on horseback. They saw where Jonah landed from his "whaling voyage," and then stayed in Sidon, named after Noah's great-grandson. They went swimming in the Sea of Galilee and later in their journey finally set up their tents outside of the walls of Jerusalem. They spent several days in Jerusalem, taking in all of the sights. Jim and William parted ways after their journey through the Holy Land. William sailed on to Australia, while Jim made his way by train.

# Chapter Six

## Down Under

The evangelist's first view of Australia came when the Mooltan, a ship of about four thousand tons, anchored for about ten hours. They stopped at Albany, at the southwest end of the continent. He heard that there was a small chapel there in town and a minister of the Church of England. There was also a man and his wife who were Wesleyans in faith. They were building a twenty-four by thirty-four foot chapel, hoping that the Wesleyan Church would send a pastor soon.

They set out from Albany for Melbourne, where Taylor lost the Captain of the ship and was now himself a stranger in a strange land. He got a room in Scott's Hotel, and set out to look for McArthur & Company. He met Mr. McArthur while he was in London, and was able to secure some contacts through his business there in Melbourne. His new friends there in the office took him to see Rev. Daniel Draper, who was Chairman of the Melbourne District. Draper had read Taylor's books on California, such as *California Life Illustrated*, and was already acquainted with the street preacher. After some discussion, both men knelt to pray, and then decided that William would preach in the pulpit of Wesley Church on Lonsdale Street.

William walked into that massive structure, noticing the difference between his first chapel back home in California, and Wesley Church. The building cost its members two hundred thousand dollars, seated over two thousand hearers, and boasted an immense organ in the rear gallery. As was his custom, Taylor preached in the morning for the regular service, and then at three that afternoon to the children of the church.

# Self-supporting Evangelist

Taylor carried on his practice of self-support there in Melbourne and all across Australia. Many wanted to give to his ministry, but he wanted the superintendent of the circuit to announce how he would refuse any money given to him. On the last day of his services, he would let the people know how they could help him. Still trying to pay off debts from the destruction of the Bethel in California, he encouraged people to purchase his books if they wanted to support his ministry.

# His Methods in Melbourne

Taylor had a weekly routine that he kept, not only in Melbourne, but also across Australia. He would preach the Gospel, and invite all unsaved people up to the front who desired to be in a right relationship with God. However, he did not make their coming forward a condition of coming to know Christ. They could surrender to God in their pews or later in their homes. He did, however, encourage the people to make their confession public.

> Then they were conducted by class leaders and introduced to the superintendent of the circuit in the vestry room adjoining the church in the rear. It was his business, according to our instructions, kindly but thoroughly to investigate each case and satisfy himself as to the genuineness of the work in each heart; and that every one who could not give a satisfactory testimony from a conscious experience of pardon and peace of God should be kindly advised to return to the altar of prayer and continue as a seeker until he should obtain a clear experience of salvation.

This method of evangelism made sure that the work was of God. Taylor took his hands off and allowed God to make the change in their hearts. If they did not feel any differently, they were directed back to the altar to pray that God would testify to their hearts that they were forgiven. When the living God comes to live inside of a dead sinner, Taylor and his contemporaries believed people would experience a difference in their lives. This teaching was brought back to life through John Wesley's heart-warming experience on Aldersgate Street. By allow-ing God to do the work, the results of an evangelist's labor was seen and felt more readily.

# Faith and Feelings

A great part of Taylor's impact had more to do with him staying out of the Spirit's way in the work of salvation. Taylor wrote in his autobiography, "When we say to a penitent soul, 'Believe that he saves you now,' suppose in point of fact he doesn't; then he is told to believe what is not true. When a poor sinner reaches the *now* when God saves him, God notifies him of his pardon by his Holy Spirit, and the Holy Spirit regenerates him, and his salvation becomes a matter of fact; not a matter of belief, but a matter of experience which he knows, and to which, as a witness, he bears testimony."

Ever since the day when John Wesley had his heart-warming experience, Methodists after him taught people that if they were truly saved, they would have experienced the Holy Spirit's presence in their lives. When someone experienced the regenerating work of the Holy Spirit through Taylor's ministry, they were then directed to go back to the churches they were members of and tell their pas-tors what had happened. Taylor did not see the need to proselytize them into his own denomination, but encouraged the new believers, that if they already belonged to a church, to stay within that church. If they were not members of a church, they gave their names and were assigned to a class that night. This would assure that the work would continue. These classes would give them an intimate family of believers where they could grow and be held accountable. Their names were then given to a class leader, and that leader was instructed to visit them in their homes and get them to a class meeting as soon as possible.

Taylor usually spent about a week in each church; however, the time would vary depending on the size of each church. Saturdays were used as a day of rest, and of traveling to the next "field of service."

# Breaking Down the Walls

Sydney during Taylor's efforts had a population around two hundred thou-sand people. He stayed with a family who were friends of his from San Francisco. His first services in Sydney were held in the York Street Church, the largest Wesleyan church in that district.

Taylor was encouraged that Christians from other churches wanted to join him in his efforts. Dr. Steele, a Scotch Presbyterian, also took an interest in Taylor's meetings. A few of the families in his church also made sure they were at many of his meetings around the city. From the very beginning, the Presbyterians entered into the work of evangelism with Taylor. One woman, Mrs. MacDonald, told Taylor during a family dinner, that she had been praying for the people of that city.

"Three months before your arrival in Sydney I was led by the good Spirit into a great struggle of prayer and fasting on behalf of the churches of this city and colony. Iniquity was abounding, and the churches were so formal and dead they seemed utterly unable to stand the opposing tide of wickedness, much less to move aggressively for the salvation of the people.

"This burden upon my heart so increased that I was unable to take sufficient sleep and food to keep me up, so that my health was sadly impaired," she continued telling Taylor. "I was led to pray specially that the Lord would send someone through whom he could stir the hearts of the people of this city and colony, and so bring them into harmony with him, so that he could use them effectively for the accomplishment of their work.

"I was finally relieved one night by a vision through a dream. I saw a beautiful chariot without any horses or any visible power of locomotion, moving slowly over the city just above the housetops, and I saw standing in it a messenger from God, a tall, straight man with a long beard, and he was sowing seed broadcast, and proclaiming in the name of the Lord. In my dream I wept for joy, and said, 'that is the man the Lord is sending in answer to my prayer.'"

The funny twist in her dream was that for months before she had been trying to get her sons to shave their long beards. She had some prejudice against men with beards.

At the time of her dream, she had never heard of Taylor. But she memorized her vision so that when she saw the man, she would know who it was who was going to be God's messenger. Three months after her vision, she learned that "Rev. William Taylor, from California, was to commence a series of special revival services in York Street Wesleyan Church." She went to the first service, and as soon as she walked through the door, she saw William standing by the pulpit, and recognized him as the man in her dream.

## Sydney Crusade

After three months work in Sydney, Taylor expressed his desire to find a hall that "would accommodate the outside masses, for whom there was no room in the churches." A man by the name of Ebenezer Vickery, offered to pay $1,500 for rent if such a hall could be found. A committee was formed and the largest auditorium that they could find was the Prince of Wales Theater, which would seat close to two thousand people.

Instead of using the theater, they decided on Hyde Park. They built a stage and a preaching stand, and lit the area with gas lamps. Due to this outdoor occasion, no seats were provided for the audience, so they stood on their feet. He preached in Hyde Park in the afternoons on two Sundays and ten week nights to a crowd that numbered anywhere from ten to seventeen thousand hearers each night. Taylor instructed them that if they wanted to give their lives to Christ, they could go to the York Street Church, "where a working force was in readiness to instruct them in the way of righteousness and lead them to the Saviour."

# His Influence

Years after his two and a half year campaign, a question was asked at the Australian Conference.

"How many of the members of this conference were converted under the labors of William Taylor?" It was then that thirty-five, one third of the entire conference stood up. Over six thousand people came to know Christ under his ministry. The amount of converts could even be more, as J. Edwin Orr reported that 6,000 were added to the Methodist Episcopal Church alone.

Other denominations grew as well. Membership in the Wesleyan Church was at its highest level. In the city of Victoria, 2,000 people came to know Christ. In Tasmania, hundreds were converted and Methodist churches doubled. John Watsford, a man who worked with Taylor, called him the greatest evangelist that ever visited Australia. No denomination was left out of the benefits of Taylor's evangelistic campaigns.

From Australia, William left his mark on the landscape of America. Seeing the four hundred foot Eucalyptus trees there, he sent some seeds to California. Being a builder himself, he thought they would be wonderful for woodworking. On the contrary, when Eucalyptus trees dry, the wood turns to dust. Although beautiful to look at, they make terrible lumber. Wherever you see a Eucalyptus tree in California, it is a testament to Taylor's work in Australia.

# The Baptist Call to India

While Taylor was touring in Victoria, he came into contact with a Baptist missionary from India by the name of Smith. Smith was able to pique Taylor's interest in India and the incredible work that needed to be done. Within that empire, there were thousands of English speaking people. William found that these people would be effective advocates, working between the English classes and the natives. Taylor decided he would work in India on his way back home to California to see his family.

# Family Reunion

All throughout his ministry he kept in touch with his family. Both Anne and William wanted to see each other all throughout his Australian work, but nothing opened up for the reunion. William wrote home to tell them of his plans to minister in India, asking whether they could join him before he left Australia. "If that is not possible, you can meet me in Bombay or Calcutta or some other center of that great country." But William got word by telegram that Anne, and his three sons, Stuart, Ross, and Edward, were all safe at the home of Dr. Moffit, a friend who lived back in Sydney.

He corresponded back to his family, telling them he had some matters to finish up in South Australia, but he cut his plans short when he received a telegram back from Anne that Stuart was running a fever. William got on the next steamer from Melbourne to Sydney.

The steamer was packed from stem to stern. The crowd that accompanied him was a wild group of men, who drank heavily and played cards for most of the trip. He had already completed two books entitled, *How to be Saved*, and *Infancy and Manhood of Christian Life*. While in the midst of the smoke, drunkenness, and course joking, he wrote his book on holiness.

William had not seen his family in four years. His heart began to race, longing to see his wife and three boys. When he caught the first glimpse of his family, he began to weep, running to embrace his wife. Ross had grown up without seeing his dad, and through the tears William swept his son up into his arms and asked, "Ross, do you know me?"

"Yes, papa," he replied.

"How did you come to know me?"

"My mother told me it was you."

Then Edward, who was only two years old when William saw him last, jumped into his daddy's arms. "Do you know me?"

"Yes, papa."

"How did you come to know me?"

"O, I remember you very well."

The family went back to Dr. Moffit's house to find Stuart in bed. Ross, Edward, and their father, went outside to pray for their brother and son. All of them prayed and wept together. Soon after their prayer meeting, Stuart began showing signs of recovery. But Dr. Moffit, in consultation with another doctor, told the Taylors that they should take the family out of Australia's hot summer, and told him that India would be no better for him.

"Stuart's only ground of hope would be to take him to South Africa. Go by sail ship, and spend the hottest part of the year in the Southern Hemisphere at sea, and arrive in Cape Town at the close of the hot season," the doctor told them.

The family went by steamer to Melbourne and then on to South Australia, where they caught the clipper ship, the St. Vincent, on its way to Cape Town, South Africa.

# Chapter Seven

## South Africa

On February 17, 1866, the Taylor family set sail from Australia. Opportunities opened up among the mission stations in South Africa for William. The Taylors landed in Table Bay, Cape of Good Hope, just as the sun was setting on March 30, 1866. At that time, the Cape Colony had a population of nearly half a million, with over 71,000 being whites.

Taylor spent the first few months preaching in Cape Town and Port Elizabeth. The churches in South Africa were much smaller than those in Australia, however, he preached all the same. The size of the church did not matter to him, for he never found it a waste of time to preach to willing listeners. But he was able to draw up a crowd by preaching on the courthouse steps, where over 600 had gathered to hear him preach.

After his sermon, one man came up to greet him and told Taylor that he had heard him on the Long Wharf in San Francisco.

"I have heard you preach to the gamblers in San Francisco and to the sailors on Long Wharf, and I heard you give a singular reproof to some sailors that I will never forget. They were loading a barge with coal, and one, with a profane oath, wished the coals in hell. 'That is quite unnecessary, my friend,' you said, 'for if you go down to that place you will find plenty of fuel.'"

What turned out to be a wrench in his plans to go to India, turned out to be a blessing for the lives God touched during his stay. His yearlong campaign took him through Cape Town, Grahams Town, King Williams Town, Queens Town, Cradock, and Somerset. He would spend a week or two in each town.

The fruit from Taylor's labors extended far beyond his preaching in revivals throughout the land. As he stayed at mission stations, many were strengthened in the faith and were led into great efforts of evangelism. On one occasion, there were three preachers in the pulpit. Taylor preached in English, another translated his words into Dutch, while still another preached in Kaffir. Missionaries reported an increase of membership of 1,200 among the colonists and 6,700 among the Kaffirs. As it did among the other nations, revival fire spread into other denominations as well. Other churches in the region recorded conversions and baptisms numbering into the hundreds.

# At Home in Wesley's House

The Taylor family then traveled to London on the steamer Norseman from Cape Town. Just a few days before Christmas, the family got a room in a hotel that faced St. Paul's Cathedral. Before moving on to India, he wanted to do some more evangelistic work in the leading Wesleyan churches.

> It was interesting to hear the songs and shouts of praise on the old battleground where John Wesley lived, labored, and died. His grave and those of…other pioneer Methodist heroes, are in the cemetery adjoining the church. The preacher's house, built by Mr. Wesley, is still in good repair, and occupied by the pastor of the church. Mr. Wesley's clock, an old-fashioned German clock, stands in a little hall at the head of the stairs. That clock has been keeping the time of the march of Methodism for more than one hundred years, and is still ticking the time of its widening way through all the zones of the globe.

John Wesley had once stated that the world was his parish. William Taylor took that statement to heart. The march of Methodism continued in Wesley's city, as Taylor began evangelistic campaigns there.

# Serving With a Soldier

During one of his preaching engagements, Catherine Booth, wife of the Salvation Army's first General and founder, William Booth, helped Taylor. At that time General Booth was starting his work among the forgotten masses who were stricken with poverty throughout the city.

During that spring, Taylor spent most of his time in the ministry, but also made the time to sightsee with his family. At one point, the Taylor boys heard that the people in Paris ate horses. As they sat down to eat, little Ross, sitting on his father's left, told his dad what he thought of the food.

"He saw me nibbling at the meat and tasting it, and he said to me, 'that's horse, papa.' I didn't certainly know whether it was horse or beef, but his remark raised a suspicion in my mind that abated my appetite for that day."

After a few more days of sightseeing, Anne took the boys to Switzerland to spend the summer, while William stayed behind to continue his work. After that summer, Anne thought it best that she move the boys back to California to continue their education and "bring them up in the Lord."

"I was not ready to return to California, and begged them not to leave me. I concurred with her judgment in relation to the education of the boys, but my great desire to be with my family rendered me quite unwilling to part with them," Taylor remembered in his autobiography. "Much of my grief grew out of sympathy with their loneliness in my absence. I was partly relieved of that source of trouble when I said to my little Eddie, "Don't you want to stop with papa, and travel England?"

"No," he said, "I want to go to California and see my dog." William consented to let them go, and so in the fall of 1867, his family went by steamer from Liverpool to New York.

# Remembered in New York

When she arrived in New York, she went to the office of the Pacific Mail Steamship Company to secure tickets for the voyage to San Francisco. Once she mentioned who she was to the man at the office, his eyes lit up and said he knew Mr. Taylor well back in California. He told her that it would be his pleasure to pay their tickets, which she accepted.

After reading her letter about the surprise gift, Taylor said, "She had perhaps in that respect more sense than her husband in that she never refused money when it was offered to her!"

# Chapter Eight

## Church Planter in India

Soon after Anne's trip to the states, and before traveling to India, William took a steamer from London to the West Indies. After many stops, Taylor was able to hold services in the islands of St. Kitts, St. Vincent, Nevis, Trinidad, Tobago, St. Thomas, and Jamaica. Taylor said the believers "were so excitable and noisy in their religious meetings that their missionaries said to me that they were afraid to preach exciting truth to their people."

William Boyce, who was a Wesleyan Missionary Secretary in London, reported that the net increase in their membership numbered to more than five thousand new members during Taylor's work there. From the West Indies Taylor traveled back to Australia in 1870, and then took a steamer from Melbourne to Ceylon. From Ceylon he took the steamship Malacca that anchored in the harbor of Bombay on November 20, 1870.

### Bombay

The Portuguese acquired the territory that is now known as Bombay in 1534. They named it Bom Bahia, which means "beautiful bay." Taylor arrived in the beautiful bay in November of 1870. Being a year shy of fifty, he began a ministry that was to reach thousands there in that country.

From Bombay, Taylor took a train to Allahabad. From there the train took him to Lucknow, and was met by a few other pastors. The Methodist Episcopal Church had opened a mission there in 1857, and had been doing a great work among the natives ever since. Over the course of a few weeks, Taylor preached to hundreds of natives. During part of his campaign, he was able to preach in English to English speaking people as well.

# Cawnpore

Cawnpore was an area outside of the Conference, and many gave their opinion that Taylor should stay within the confines of the Conference. But he wouldn't hear of such a thing. He brought the matter to God in prayer, and all his doubts were removed about taking up a work there. From the very start he was given clues that the journey was of God and not of his own volition. One of those clues came as he was looking for a family friend.

While he was back in Sydney, his friend Dr. Moffit wanted him to visit his nephew, another Dr. Moffit. When he could not find the man's home, his driver knew where Dr. Moffatt lived and took him there, thinking it was the same man. But when he walked up to the door, it was obviously not the same doctor. However, this Dr. Moffatt had been to India as a surgeon of "her majesty's Fourteenth Regiment," and had opened a way for missions work to be done in Cawnpore.

From that point on Taylor decided not to make any plans. He realized that instead of asking God to bless his efforts that he would do what God was blessing.

"I see more and more clearly that it is too late for me to begin to make plans for the Lord by which to work, when God has so long ago made plans for me. It is not mine to ask him to indorse my plans and go with me, but by all available means to discern his plans and go with him."

During Taylor's work in Cawnpore, twenty-two East Indians came to know Christ. He had organized them into two bands at each of the preaching places. He was able to show a few other presiding elders the work there so that they could present the idea at Conference of having a permanent mission. Later the Conference voted to do just that, and added Cawnpore into the circuit. One year later the mission became the first self-supporting mission in the Conference.

# Putting Out the Fires

Taylor then moved on to Panahpore. When his time to preach came during that week, a sudden announcement was heard that a fire was spreading through the jungle. Because he had experience in fighting fires back in Virginia, he was able to be a great help to the people. An old Brahman had a farm that was in the way of the fire. Taylor went down to assist the old man and his laborers. When they succeeded in putting out the fire, Taylor succeeded in putting out the fires of hell in their lives, for sixteen women and five men came to know Christ that night.

His preaching came with results in Panahpore. He preached in an orphanage of about 120 children, and was able to preach in homes as well. During his short stay, he organized a church in the house of a brother Walker.

# Back in Bombay

The people of Bombay worshipped one God, but did it through the medium of the elements, their favorite being fire. During the fifteen hundred mile trip to Bombay, William took some time to study the language and the character of the people.

He spent time in a few towns that surrounded Bombay. The doors of the Free Church of Scotland were open to him on a few occasions. Up until that time, Bombay did not have her own Methodist Episcopal Church. Taylor's work had stirred many hearts, one of which wrote him to express his enthusiasm in the work of planting a church in Bombay.

> To the Reverend William Taylor, Dear Brother, We, the under-signed, who have by God's mercy been awakened through your preaching to a sense of our sins, and who have found the Lord Jesus to be our Deliverer, are desirous for the establishment of a Methodist Episcopal Church in this city. We are satisfied, from all that we have yet learned, of the scriptural authority for the methods practiced by the Church to which you belong; and we therefore unitedly invite you to take the necessary steps for the accomplishment of our wishes, and to act yourself as our pastor and evangelist until such time as you can make arrangements with the Home Board for sending out the necessary agency to this city.

The signers of the letter numbered eighty-three. William responded enthusiastically to their request. He wrote them, saying that he was bound by his loyalty to Christ to concur with them on this movement.

> After I received your letter I read to the fellowship bands the General Rules of our societies, that all might know from the start the self-denying, cross-bearing life necessary to constitute a true Methodist—that is, to find out God's Gospel *methods* and pursue them with a martyr spirit of fidelity to him and to mankind. So our organization has now become a matter of history. Let it be distinctly understood that we do not wish to hinder, but to help, the spiritual progress of all pre-existing churches in this great country.

In 1872, it was unanimously decided by the Conference that this church in Bombay would be fully self-supporting, and that it would not take any drafts from the Missionary Society. The church was to "be led directly by the Holy Spirit of God and supported by him from Indian resources." Taylor felt beyond a shadow of any doubt, every mission agency should have it as its goal to be self-supporting.

> All admit that self-support is, or should be, the earnest aim of every mission. If a work in India, the same as in England or America, can start on this healthy, sound principle, is it not better than a long, sickly, dependent pupilage, which in too many instances amounts to pauperism? I am not speaking of missionaries, but of mission churches. We simply wish to stand on the same platform exactly as our churches in America, which began poor and worked their way up by their own industry and liberality, without funds from the Missionary Society.

## The Growing Attraction

The church in Bombay was growing in many respects, with people coming to know Christ through the lives of those who were changed from the inside out.

"Salam, babu!"

"Salam, sahib!"

"What is your religion?" asked Commissioner Drummond.

"I am a Hindu," replied the young man.

"What have you come here for?"

"To hear Padri Taylor, sahib."

"He's not a Hindu; why do you come to hear him?"

"Well, sahib, there is a very mysterious work going on here in connection with his meetings. Many men, whom I knew to be drunkards, swearers, and dishonest men, tyrannical men, too, who were before always abusing the natives in their employ, have been entirely changed at these meetings. They are now all teetotalers; they are honest and true in their dealings, and speak nothing but words of kindness to everybody; and instead of hating and abusing their servants they show real love and sympathy for them and are all the time trying to do them good. I have looked into these things closely, and know that what I tell you, sahib, is true; and this kind of work is going on all the time at Padri Taylor's meetings. I don't understand it, but I feel so anxious to know more about it that I can't keep away."

Many were being attracted to Christ by the changed lives of their friends. Maybe Taylor had a way in which he communicated that would draw up a crowd, but in a city where more people spoke a language other than English, Christ was gathering the community of Bombay to the community of believers. One man was surprised to see that his nephews, after becoming Christians, looked the same as before.

He surveyed the boys closely, and in a soft voice said, "Why, you look just as you looked when I saw you last!" The man expected to see them dressed in European clothing.

"Our missionary is different from any you know," they replied. "He don't require us to change any outward custom, but simply to give up all idolatry and sin." Many mission agencies of the time brought in Western culture as much as they brought in Christ. But Taylor only wished to see a change of heart. And those changed hearts went out to help change the Hindus.

# Calcutta

Before Taylor arrived in Calcutta, there was one Methodist church with eighteen members. During Taylor's time the city numbered over six million. Taylor was given the suggestion that he limit his work to the Wesleyan Chapel, a suggestion he did not care to entertain.

Taylor secured the use of halls all across the city, holding weekly services for families six or seven times a day. He began working with a Baptist pastor, the principal of a native boys school that had over two hundred students. The school had a forty by sixty foot chapel.

"I don't know what this chapel was built for except the anticipation of getting many of the native students to become Christians, which, I am sorry to say, has not been realized," pastor Kerry told Taylor. "We have a small native congregation and church which worships here at 7a.m. and 4p.m. Beyond that we have no use for it, and if you can make any use of it you are welcome to it."

Taylor replied, "It is really not that well located for my English-speaking East Indians, but there is not really any other place available. I am sure this is where God wants us. Thank you. Let's make some quick preparations. We will advertise and hold services here." Kerry did a lot to advance the work with Taylor, but both found it very difficult. Taylor admitted that the hardest work he had ever done was on the streets of Calcutta.

> I became more and more convinced that a great work of God was what Calcutta least desired and most needed, and that a more convenient season would never come; so I determined, as the Lord should lead, to push the battle and win or die at the guns....God has sent me here to organize at least one body of witnessing soldiers for Jesus who will endure hardness; and by the power of the Holy Spirit I must succeed or die in the trenches of the enemy. God help me! It is for thy glory and the salvation of these poor, perishing millions, in love and pity for whom my Saviour died.

After two months of hard work, thirteen people came to know Christ and presented themselves as candidates for membership in his church. He appointed a Dr. Thoburn to be their pastor, and moved on to Madras.

# Madras

Madras is a city located on the eastern shore, on the Bay of Bengal. The territory was settled in 1693. A church, named the Cathedral of San Thome, was built over the place where the Apostle Thomas was buried. The population at the time Taylor arrived was close to four hundred thousand, most of which were Hindus. There were eighty-six members in the Methodist church there, and it was Taylor's desire to plant another work within the city of Madras.

Taylor led evangelistic services in halls across the city, including a Baptist chapel for three months. He moved a group of people from Evangelistic Hall to Memorial Hall, which reminded him of the Exeter Hall in London. It seated some six hundred people, and was filled four nights out of the week for four weeks. His method was the same in Madras as it was in other cities:

> Each night of our services I wrote down the name and address of each person professing to find Jesus, and next day, or as soon as possible, called to see the converts. Those whom I found to be connected with the Baptists or Wesleyans, or wherever they were likely to be well cared for and do good, I advised to remain, and discontinued my pastoral visits to such, amounting to perhaps a couple of hundred persons; but all such were not actual members of any Church, or merely nominal members, especially of ritualistic Churches, with not much probability of pastoral nurture such as they needed, I organized into fellowship bands in private houses.

Within a month of Taylor's arrival, there were eight fellowship bands meeting on five different days all across the city. Then for five or six months after they were formed, Taylor would lead all of them personally until he could develop leaders for them from among their own people. He did not call in other pastors, but rose up leaders right from within his own bands. A few months later, these bands were able to raise sufficient funds to build a chapel, which measured forty six by sixty seven feet.

# Telegram from D.L. Moody

After Madras, Taylor found the same kind of success in Bangalore, where he was able to establish another circuit and appoint a pastor from Bombay. He went from there to Lahore to help his "Presbyterian brethren," where he received a letter from London.

> Mr. Moody has requested me to write to you, in the hope that the Lord may give you to hear in this invitation the cry, "Come over and help us." Of course all expenses will be guaranteed. I may remind you that London is the metropolis of the world, and that to move this mighty city as it never has been moved is worth any effort which any number of men of God can put forth….We fervently hope that it may be our Father's good pleasure to appoint you as one of his ambassadors in this great work.

The letter was signed by R.C. Morgan, editor for *The Christian.* Taylor did not know whether to go at first because of his work in India. He wanted to keep pushing on there, but decided that he could go to London for four months in connection with seeing his family. The letter was reprinted in the February 27, 1875 issue of the *Bombay Guardian.*

# The Results

A measure of a man's work cannot be seen when he is in that place of work, but when he leaves it. After Taylor left his mission in Calcutta, the church that he planted swelled to over six hundred people. When Taylor arrived in that city the Methodists had a voice of eighteen members. A London circular commented on Taylor's mission, saying:

> Its present working force comprises twelve ordained and twelve lay preachers, devoted wholly to evangelistic and pastoral work, and thirteen hundred members and workers, who support their own ministers and pay all running expenses of their work except their pioneer superintendent, who refuses to take a penny from them…. He maintains firmly the Bible doctrine that the laborer is worthy of his hire, and that as a rule all ministers and missionaries should be supported by the voluntary funds of the people; but Paul, as a pioneer, chose to forego his rights and build tents; so Mr. Taylor sees it best for him in his world-wide range as an evangelist to proceed on St. Paul's principle, using books instead of tents.

Through Taylor's ministry, what had been only a few voices in the Methodist church in India, multiplied to make up two new conferences: The South India Conference and the North India Conference. His work was not only evangelistic, but he planted churches as well. Following Wesley's model of the Class Meetings, people who were recently converted under Taylor's ministry would enter these "small groups," or fellowship bands for encouragement, challenge and support. In February of 1872, at the request of these Class Meetings, Taylor organized a Methodist congregation in Bombay. Then throughout India, the same movement began in other cities. *The Encyclopedia of World Methodism* stated that the list of cities where Taylor planted churches was too numerous to list.

It was there in India that Taylor developed the "Pauline Method of Missions." This was the mark of his life already, stemming back to his prayer in California.

As the fellowship bands requested to be formed into churches, they were organized to undertake the support of their own pastors. These churches would then become the center for evangelization of other English-speaking people, as well as reaching into the native population.

# Chapter Nine

## Preacher Turns Teacher

Taylor had not seen his family in over seven years. After spending time with them back in California, he felt called to begin missions in South America. He arrived in Callao, Peru, in 1877. While he spent time with European settlers, Taylor noticed that they were more interested in education than evangelism. Instead of leaving because a lack of interest in evangelism, Taylor recruited teacher-preachers to man the mission centers. His Pauline Principles were carried over, as the mission centers became fully funded by the local residents.

### Starting Schools

The Arequipa and Puno railway line employed a large number of English speaking mechanics in Mollendo, which was a far five hundred miles away from Callao, Peru. He arrived in Mollendo on Saturday, January 5, 1878. He visited a small congregation that night before preaching the next day, and found that his strategy needed to change to reach these people.

He wrote a letter back proposing the agency send him a schoolteacher, "being also a Gospel minister." As he spoke with a number of the people, he found that the only way he could reach them was to first lay a foundation through education. Thus the church sent Taylor a man by the name of Magnus Smith, who was a graduate of Williams College in Massachusetts. He had a few years of German studies under his belt. However, his first attempt at setting up a school failed, for the young teacher-preacher "fell asleep in the arms of Jesus" due to lung disease.

# Tacna, Peru

From his contacts in Callao, Taylor learned that the people of Tacna were an enterprising people. So he made his way there and received a warm welcome. He discussed with a number of people in that town his prospect of setting up a school, but he did not receive any encouragement until a discussion with a German man.

"There are a few English and German families here in Tacna, and I believe that a good English school is one of the great needs of this city," informed Taylor's new friend.

"Well sir, I am very glad I met up with you. You have done me good."

Taylor returned to his room, but being the visionary that he was, he could not fall asleep. God raced ideas through his mind and was able to help him discern the direction of how to reach out to the people of Tacna. He knew that he had to send in teachers instead of preachers, because the latter would not be very accepted. So instead of staying to plant a church, his first matter of business was to bring in educators who could lay a foundation for further church planting.

Taylor wrote, "Tacna was to be my first departure from the old lines of purely evangelistic work to the new line of school work simply, where nothing more is at present possible."

Taylor had the plan mapped out before morning, and was able to meet the merchants the next day to raise support for this new school. Before the day was done, Taylor had raised enough support to bring in two teachers, one male and one female, for at least three years.

After he had secured Tacna as a center for English education, he moved on to Iquique, Chile. On January 17, of 1878, he proposed to the people of that city the same request he made in Tacna.

On that same day, Taylor received this reply: "We, the undersigned, concur in Mr. Taylor's proposal, and agree to pay the sums we here subscribe, and do all else we can to make the undertaking a success."

This letter had the signatures of fifty names on it, securing another success of bringing in another teacher for at least three years. By the time Taylor arrived in New York in June of that same year, he learned that the money for the teachers had already been collected and sent ahead to secure their passage.

# Remembered in Chile

Taylor began to lay the foundation for a mission station in Antofagasta, which had nearly ten thousand residents. Then he built a bethel in Valparaiso. Much like his bethel in San Francisco, this was a place where lonely sailors would be welcomed. Valparaiso was the home to eighty thousand people. It was founded by the Spanish in 1536, and began to grow after Chile gained its independence in 1818. In 1876, the city grew by twenty five hundred people, and another four thousand made it their home in 1877. It was growing fast due to its use as a port of call for ships rounding Cape Horn. This port served as perfect ground for Taylor's ministry to seamen.

William stayed with a man by the name of Dr. Trumball. Trumball had connections with many of the leading men of the city, which gave William a great opportunity to run his idea of a school by them. On a February afternoon in '78, William Laurence and his wife welcomed Taylor. They met with another man, Henry Bunster, who Taylor later called his "providential man for that moment." Bunster was in town on other business, but was able to meet with Taylor to hear his request.

The man lit up and excitedly exclaimed, "I know who you are. I heard you preach on the Plaza in San Francisco many times. I will never forget those days." Taylor showed him his book written about that ministry, and Bunster put in $50 for the school. From there they met with other leading men of the city and were able to raise enough support to guarantee the success of opening a school there in Valparaiso.

Taylor ran into similar success in other cities throughout South America. In Talca his people were able to open up a college. In Santiago a church was established as well as a Female College. Taylor was able to work with his brother in Callao, Peru. He admitted that his brother was an "able Gospel preacher."

He opened twelve centers of education and evangelization within the boarders of South America, and hired a man to do his recruiting for these schools. Among the qualifications for these teachers, Taylor wanted them to be able singers and vocal teachers. The men and women sent were extremely gifted in those areas. As he was heading home, he wrote *Our South American Cousins*, which gave more details of his work there. Through the sale of those books, he personally sent teachers into this new area. By 1892, six of the schools had an enrollment that totaled 957 students.

# Chapter Ten

# Bishop of Africa

After visiting India to strengthen his missions there, he came back to the states to join the General Conference in 1884. It was there in Philadelphia that Taylor was nominated with great enthusiasm as Missionary Bishop for Africa. Though he was 63, he devoted twelve strong years.

The people of Africa called him "the flaming torch," as he brought them the light of Jesus' message. They also called him the "well-digger," for he taught the natives how to dig for water instead of wasting their energies on carrying it from the distant springs.

It was from this nation that the author-turned-publisher gave America *The African News*. This was a monthly magazine that followed the events of Taylor's ministry throughout Africa. Much like Billy Graham's *Discover Magazine*, *The African News* outlined the evangelist's work and gave inspiring stories from the Word of God.

One of the stories in the magazine asked, "Shall the devil with his rum and licentiousness overrun this vast country before Christians get even a foothold there? Bishop William Taylor, as the Gideon of the nineteenth century, heads a little army that God has specially chosen, and says *NO!*" In a four-year time span, Bishop William Taylor had sent one hundred missionaries into the deep dark heart of Africa. Taylor funded and built a steamer to bring missionaries and supplies through the Congo.

There were some special characteristics of these missions. One, they were, as other missions were, self-supporting. Missionaries were to come up with their own money to pay their transit, plus funds to feed them during the first year when the crops would come up. They would then live off the crops from then on.

The second characteristic was that the missionaries were not to go in to the country as rich people backed by a rich country. They were to go in poor so that they would live among the natives, and be accepted by them. They were to go in simply with the love and message of Jesus Christ.

A third characteristic was that they would bring in the technology of civilization, but the natives were to be partners in this endeavor. The native ruler gave many acres of each mission station for the work of harvesting crops. The missionaries, while encouraging the natives to work side by side with them, worked the fields. The missionaries would teach by example. They would learn the skills to work the land for themselves.

Another feature of his work was that it was not confined to ordained ministry. Teachers and other workers were made to feel like they were co-workers with God.

# Chapter Eleven

## Retirement and Promotion

In 1896, Bishop Taylor retired from the General Conference. It was at the Northwest Iowa Conference that Rev. Bennet Michel heard him, saying,

"Bishop Taylor was in feeble health, yet able to give in his own peculiar way an account of his travels in the Dark Continent. It was an inspiration to hear his apostolic words and to look into his saintly face. He was tall, a little stooped by age, with a long flowing beard and eagle eyes that peered forth from beneath heavy, over-shadowing brows...his language was like Jesus and like Him he got the attention of the people and held it."

All throughout the world, William Taylor left a mark in the hearts and minds of those who heard him. From there, Taylor moved back to his home in Palo Alto, California. Then in 1902, William Taylor was promoted to glory.

The May 19th issue of the *San Francisco Chronicle* records these words: "He went into a state of coma Friday night, from which he never emerged. On Tuesday he had said, 'I am nearing the shore.' Back in April he predicted that his death would occur within a few weeks, and he said he was only waiting patiently for the summons."

The summons came at a family home with Anne by his side. He is buried at Mountain View Cemetery in Oakland, California. Mrs. Taylor chose the spot on the mountainside to be a reminder. Mrs. Taylor said, as people look at "the beauty of the scene and wide scope of the horizon, and view of San Francisco, the Golden Gate and ocean," They would be reminded of the "wide expanse of Williams Taylor's work and the exquisite charm of his personality."

## Taylor University

Though buried on a hill in California, William Taylor's life is celebrated in the cornfields of Upland, Indiana and the city streets of Fort Wayne, Indiana. On July 11, 2003, Taylor graduates gathered at his graveside to dedicate a plaque placed there. It reads,

> Bishop William Taylor was one of the first Methodist Missionaries to reach California, where he ministered to miners, Native Americans and sailors. He later traveled the globe supporting himself by writing books and sharing Christ wherever he went. His life of faith was so closely aligned with the mission of Fort Wayne College in Indiana that in 1890, the trustees of the school agreed to rename the institution Taylor University. To this day, the institution, with campuses in Upland and Fort Wayne, Indiana, continues to prepare men and women to follow in the footsteps of its namesake, ministering the love of Christ to a world in need.

Even in death his life speaks of what a man or woman can do when they live a life with the purpose, power and passion like this pioneer prophet.

0-595-29134-1